Origami
for the first time®

"Wings of Love" folded by Soonboke Smith and arranged by Martin Lovato

Origami
for the first time®

Soonboke Smith

Sterling Publishing Co., Inc.
New York
A Sterling/Chapelle Book

Chapelle, Ltd.

Jo Packham
Sara Toliver
Cindy Stoeckl

Editor: Leslie Farmer
Contributing Writer: Geoline Havener
Photography: Kevin Dilley for Hazen Photography
Photo Stylist: Suzy Skadburg
Editorial Director: Caroll Shreeve
Art Director: Karla Haberstich
Copy Editor: Marilyn Goff
Graphic Illustrator: Kim Taylor
Staff: Burgundy Alleman, Kelly Ashkettle, Areta Bingham,
    Ray Cornia, Emily Frandsen, Lana Hall, Susan Jorgensen,
    Barbara Milburn, Lecia Monsen, Desirée Wybrow

Library of Congress Cataloging-in-Publication Data Available

(HB) 10 9 8 7 6 5 4 3 2
(PB) 10 9 8 7 6 5

Published in paperback 2004
by Sterling Publishing Co., Inc.
387 Park Avenue South, New York, NY 10016
©2003 by Soonboke Smith
Distributed in Canada by Sterling Publishing
c/o Canadian Manda Group, One Atlantic Avenue, Suite 105
Toronto, Ontario, Canada M6K 3E7
Distributed in Great Britain by Chrysalis Books Group PLC
The Chrysalis Building, Bramley Road, London W10 6SP, England
Distributed in Australia by Capricorn Link (Australia) Pty. Ltd.
P.O. Box 704, Windsor, NSW 2756, Australia
Printed in China
All Rights Reserved

Sterling ISBN 0-8069-7867-8 Hardcover
    ISBN 1-4027-1767-9 Paperback

Write Us

If you have any questions or comments, please contact:
Chapelle, Ltd., Inc.,
P.O. Box 9252, Ogden, UT 84409
(801) 621-2777 • (801) 621-2788 Fax
e-mail: chapelle@chapelleltd.com
web site: chapelleltd.com

"Whispers of Pure Love" folded by Soonboke Smith and arranged by Martin Lovato

Table of Contents

Section 1:

Origami Basics—10

Section 2:

Basic Techniques—36

Section 3:

Beyond the Basics—56

Photo by Michael Skarsten

"Mirror to My Heart" developed by Soonboke Smith
and arranged by Martin Lovato

Section 4:

The Gallery—98

Introduction

The art of paper folding began long before paper was invented. Asian and Polynesian peoples are known to have created ceremonial and utilitarian handicrafts by folding and weaving ti leaves, palm fronds, and pounded mulberry bark.

Recently discovered ancient paper fragments would suggest that paper has only been in use in Asia during the last few thousand years. Specimens of a rudimentary hemp paper product from the Western Han Dynasty (206 B.C. to 24 A.D.) were discovered in Jinguan and Shaanxi areas of China. Eastern Han Dynasty imperial court administrator, Cai Lun, is credited with refining the papermaking process in 105 A.D. Since that time, however, paper has been widely used by Asian peoples as a mode for artistic, intellectual, and spiritual expression as well as a means for documenting day-to-day business.

It is only in the last 200 years, as people from Asia emigrated to the west, that the ancient art of paper folding, as well as other traditional Asian arts and crafts, made its appearance in Europe and America.

Though oriental communities all over the world still fold paper for ceremonial and utilitarian purposes and the Polynesians continue the art of ti folding, the root of this art form has influenced others and spawned new ones. For example, a form of flat modular paper folding called "tea bag folding" was recently developed in Holland. Tea bag folding, which resembles geometric quilting and is used to decorate greeting cards, frames, memory books, and many other contemporary crafts, has since spread all over Europe and America.

The art of folding paper has become more diverse in its artistic complexity as world cultures have begun to mingle in the last century. In the west, the art of folding paper is more commonly known as "origami," the Japanese word for folding paper. The word origami lends itself to the almost magical metamorphosis that paper undergoes as it is folded into fanciful shapes. Origami literally translates into paper (ori) and magical spirit (gami or kami).

The magical quality of folding paper into enchanting objects makes origami a powerful educational and therapeutic tool. Schoolteachers use origami as a fun way to teach subjects like geometry, science, and oriental culture. Physical therapists use origami to help clients develop hand strength and fine hand motor skills. Counseling therapists use origami to teach clients relaxation techniques and also to break the ice with those who are reluctant to interact.

Origami utilizes a wide variety of paper and non-paper products for a myriad of purposes. Paper products include traditional precut origami paper, handmade art paper, lithographic paper, office supply paper, party paper, and scrap paper from magazines, calendars, and telephone books. More durable materials such as fabric, thin malleable metals, plastics, and other foldable materials make lasting handicrafts for home decor, jewelry, gifts, and parties. In the culinary world, origami techniques are utilized in creative presentation of foods and elegant cloth or paper napkin settings. Something about origami brings a sense of tranquil beauty to all types of contemporary arts and crafts. Origami has grown from an oriental craft to an international one.

How to use this book

Origami for the first time® combines ancient yet simple origami techniques to create a wide variety of decorative items for the home, parties, culinary decor, seasonal decor, fanciful gift items, etc. The possibilities are virtually endless.

Section 1: Origami Basics will introduce you to an eclectic array of tools, supplies, papers, and non-paper products. You will also learn how to make basic origami folds and forms—the foundations of nearly all origami figures.

Section 2: Basic Techniques will teach you how to use simple folding techniques to create seven quick-and-easy projects. Once you have mastered these pieces, you will be able to handle more difficult ones.

Section 3: Beyond the Basics features 16 projects that require more-complex folding and assembling techniques.

Section 4: The Gallery presents a collection of origami pieces to demonstrate the high level of sculptural artistry that can be accomplished and the stylish crafts that are being produced by innovative origami crafts professionals.

The primary intent of this book is to teach basic origami techniques to let you gain the experience and desire to move on and use your own creative spirit to incorporate these techniques into designing origami pieces for yourself, your family, friends, craft fairs, work, play, and even your community.

Once you start origami, you will find how meditative, addicting, and socializing it can become. The portability of small pieces of paper makes origami a craft that can be done not only at home but while waiting at an office, at a shopping mall, at an airport, at a restaurant, on a plane, on a bus, or wherever and whenever time permits. The ability to transform simple pieces of paper into something beautiful through folding also makes origami an inexpensive, yet powerful crafting technique that you can start learning, creating, and experimenting with right now. Soon you will be able to graduate to more-challenging materials and origami folds.

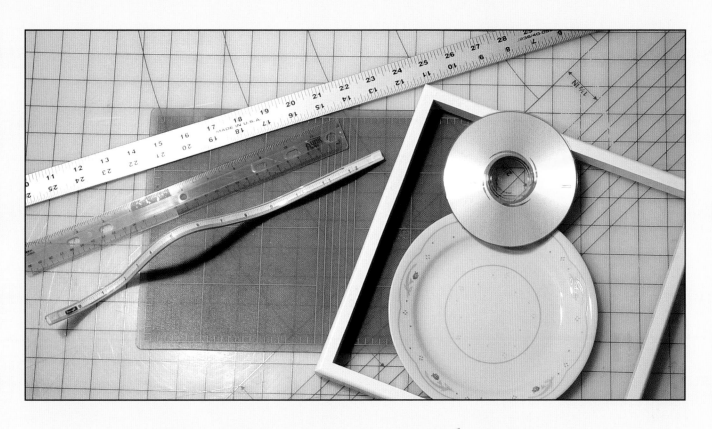

Section 1: origami basics

What do I need to get started?

Although all you really need to get started is a square sheet of paper and your fingers, the following list of tools, products, and materials will help to further enhance your first-time origami experience.

Cutting Tools

Rotary Trimmer

Rotary trimmers are great for cutting all types of paper stock and they work especially well with rolled paper as the pressure strip helps to keep the paper flat while cutting. (See Photo A) Some manufacturers offer interchangeable decorative-edged rotary blades that make patterned cuts that will add pizzazz to some of your origami creations. There is also a scoring blade that works well for scoring card stock and cover stock for heavier projects.

Hand-held Rotary Cutter

Hand-held rotary cutters will cut both paper and fabric. (See Photo B) You will need a cutting mat and a hard straightedge like a metal ruler to help hold down and trim the paper or fabric. If you will be using your rotary cutter for both fabric and paper, remember that fabric requires a sharp blade. Use older, duller blades on paper to make the best use of your rotary blades. Blades for these cutters are also available in an assortment of decorative edges.

Craft Scissors

Craft scissors are necessary for reducing large sheets or rolls of paper or fabric into more manageable sizes so that you can use rotary trimmers and cutters. (See Photo C) Scissors are also used for cutting nonstandard folding shapes. Smaller, sharp-pointed scissors are used for fine-detail cutting.

Decorative-edged Scissors

Decorative-edged scissors provide another way to make patterned cuts on your paper. (See Photo C)

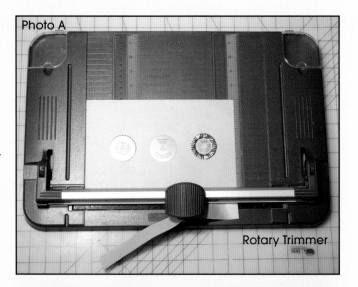

Photo A
Rotary Trimmer

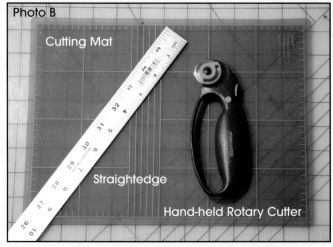

Photo B
Cutting Mat
Straightedge
Hand-held Rotary Cutter

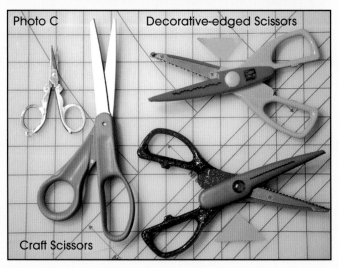

Photo C
Decorative-edged Scissors
Craft Scissors

Other Methods for Trimming Paper

Tearing

Tearing is a great way to create a soft edge on your paper. It is also the only option in those times when all you have is letterhead paper and your hands. The best way to tear paper is by creasing it, bending it forward and back several times on the crease, and holding the paper along the crease with the thumb and index finger of one hand while you tear with the other hand.

Professional Cutting Machines

Professional cutting machines are available for use at copying, printing, and binding centers for cutting entire reams of paper. All types of fancy printed, mulberry, India, and vellum papers are now available by the ream in letter size and larger. Purchasing and professionally cutting paper by the ream is an economical way to obtain beautiful paper squares at a fraction of the cost of traditional origami paper.

Measuring & Shaping Tools

Measuring Grids

Measuring grids are normally imprinted on rotary trimmers and cutting mats. (See Photo D)

Measuring Sticks

Measuring sticks come in many lengths. (See Photo D) Some are also flexible and can be used for tracing rounded curves on corners. Metal measuring sticks, also called straightedges, are not only useful for measuring but are essential when using a rotary cutter for safer, quicker, and cleaner paper cutting.

Templates

Templates can be found in many sizes and forms. (See Photo D) Discarded computer CDs make great circular templates while box frames make wonderful square templates. Other objects such as cake pans, plates, etc., can be used as templates. Templates also can be made from card, cover, and poster-board stocks.

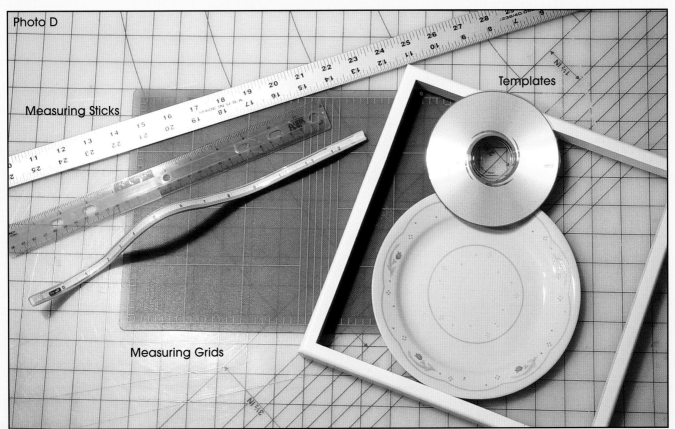

Photo D

Measuring Sticks

Templates

Measuring Grids

Creasing Tools

Fingers

Your fingers are essential for making sharp creases. On a flat surface like a tabletop, desk, or large book, you can hold the folded sheet down with one hand and smooth down the line of the fold with a little pressure from the index finger of the other hand (or both index and middle fingers depending on how thick or thin the material is).

You can also create a crease by pinching the paper between your thumb and index finger and sliding them along the line of the fold. This method also helps to relax an open crease or create a light curl in the paper.

Scoring Blades & Bone Folders

Scoring blades and bone folders can be used to score precreases into heavy-paper stock. (See Photo E) Scoring blades are used with rotary trimmers to create a precrease. When using a bone folder to score heavy-paper stock, place a straightedge on the heavy-paper stock where the precrease is desired and slide the tip of the bone folder along the straightedge. To create a sharp precrease, lay the scored paper on a hard flat surface, make the fold, and slide the flat edge of the bone folder along the fold.

Pushing Tools

Long needles, wooden skewers, and opened paper clips are some examples of tools that are useful for gently pushing folded corners and points out. (See Photo E) These tools become especially useful when folding tiny pieces of origami.

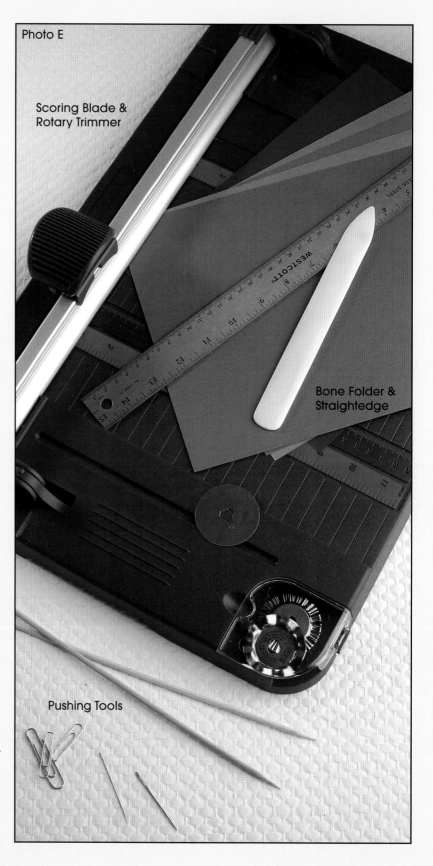

Photo E

Scoring Blade & Rotary Trimmer

Bone Folder & Straightedge

Pushing Tools

Decorative Tools

Paints

Generally, dry-brush painting and stenciling used sparingly may liven up the appearance of paper. Spray paints and spray glitters also can be applied sparingly to paper products and origami. (See Photo F) Paints should be tested on scrap paper to ensure that the paint does not destroy or warp the integrity of the paper used in the origami project. Always pretest when using any type of paint or wet glitter product.

Rubber Stamps

Rubber stamping with quick-drying inks and paints allows you to create your own paper prints, patterns, and greetings. (See Photo F) As with painting, make certain your inks do not warp the integrity of the paper by pretesting the product.

Paper Punches

Paper punches are great for creating fancy edges and corners on paper. (See Photo F)

Mounting Tools

Wire & Wire Cutters

Wires are often used by origami museums to mount small pieces of origami. Straight floral wire is especially useful for mounting origami. Wire cutters or an old pair of scissors are necessary for cutting wire. You may also use needle-nosed pliers to bend wire when mounting origami to jewelry projects. (See Photo G)

Straight Pins

Straight pins can be used to secure origami to corkboard, cork coasters, sponges, floral foam, soft woods, etc. (See Photo G)

Wooden Dowels

Wooden dowels also can be utilized like wire to mount origami for display purposes. (See Photo G)

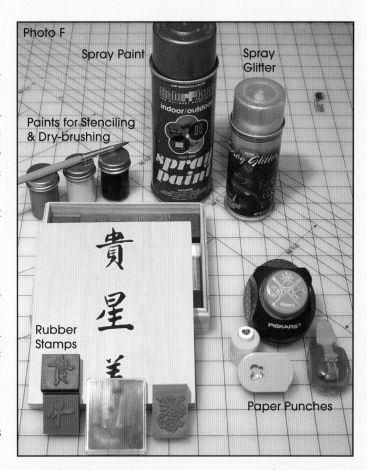

Photo F — Spray Paint, Spray Glitter, Paints for Stenciling & Dry-brushing, Rubber Stamps, Paper Punches

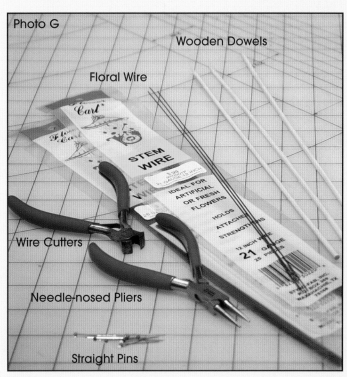

Photo G — Wooden Dowels, Floral Wire, Wire Cutters, Needle-nosed Pliers, Straight Pins

Glues & Clips

Glues are used for constructing complex pieces and for mounting origami to other surfaces for decorative purposes. (See Photo H) A craft glue stick can take care of most places where a bit of glue is needed. Rubber cement is great for temporary card mounting and does not curl or warp paper. Fast-drying white tacky glue is great for mounting origami permanently to many types of surfaces. Hot glue is a great timesaver when using origami to decorate large wreaths and other craft projects. Industrial-bond adhesives are great for more-stubborn papers like foils; for slick surfaces like glass, marble, tile, and metals; or for leather and fabrics. Jeweler's glue is great for mounting beads, gems, and rhinestones to origami as it dries crystal clear and creates a very solid bond.

Pinch-clips and hemostats are useful when anchoring compound origami pieces together while the glue cures. (See Photo H)

Fixatives & Sealers

Spray fixatives and sealers are used to preserve the surface of an origami project. (See Photo I) Spray acrylics and polyurethane glosses work to preserve and to stiffen origami creations made from paper. You should always pretest the product to make certain that the spray will not destroy or warp the integrity of the material.

Photo H

White Tacky Glue

Craft Glue Stick

Industrial-bond Adhesives

Pinch-clips

Jeweler's Glue

Rubber Cement

Hot-glue Gun & Glue Sticks

Photo I

Polyurethane Gloss

Spray Acrylic

16

Origami Papers (See Photo J)

Japanese Washi (beautiful kimono prints on special handmade paper)

Precut packaged origami papers:
- Commons
- Double-sided
- Patterned
- Textured

Common Papers (See Photo K)

Card stocks
Doilies
Foils
Letterhead papers
Money
Wrapping papers

Other Papers (See Photo L)

Coffee filters
Construction papers
Crepe papers
Newspaper pages
Magazine pages
Party napkins
Telephone book pages
Twisted-paper raffia
Wallpapers

Fabrics (See Photo M)

Bandannas
Fabric napkins
Origami mesh
Quilting squares

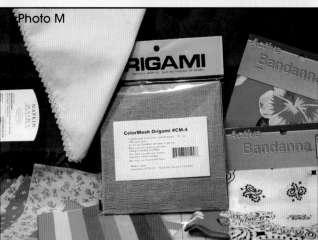

What terms and symbols do I need to know?

Terms

Basic folds, basic forms

Basic folds are the common techniques used to make different basic forms. An original origami project is the result of specific variations, or events, added onto one of these basic forms. Thus, several different origami projects can share the same basic form which is made up of a common set of preliminary folds. Once you learn how to accomplish the basic forms, you will simply refer back to them each time we begin a new project. This way we can save time and space by not having to repeat instructions. The names given to these basic forms, or bases, may sometimes vary from one origami instructor to the next. Some instructors simply number their basic forms.

Crease, precrease

Sharp creases make a big difference in the final appearance of an origami model. Precreases are soft creases that make folding paper along a crease line easier to see and do as a set of folding techniques progresses.

Kami

This Japanese term has evolved in origami groups to refer to origami paper squares. You may hear this word come up from time to time in origami groups.

Mountain fold, peak fold

This is a convex crease, or fold.

Pleats, pleating

This is a folding technique that requires a series of convex and concave creases, or folds. It is used to shape delicate curves into origami.

Score, scoring

A bone folder and straightedge or rotary scoring blades are used to lightly etch a crease line into a piece of heavy-paper stock in order to make a clean, sharp precrease or fold.

Stair-step fold, zigzag fold, accordion fold, fan fold, shell fold

These are all three-dimensional folding techniques that require a series of convex and concave folds.

Valley fold

This is a concave crease, or fold.

Washi

Washi is a specialty handmade Japanese paper that can be found at origami stores, specialty art stores, Japanese bookstores, and some craft stores in full, half, and quarter sheets as well as in precut origami squares. Larger sheets of beautiful washi paper make excellent Japanese doll kimonos. Precut washi squares have names like chiyogami, kozogami, yuzen, mingei, wazome, unryu, tanabata, katagumo, and others to denote a type of paper process, printing style, or design style of paper. Washi paper is also called Japanese art paper at specialty art stores.

Wet-folding

Wet-folding is an origami paper-sculpting technique in which you lightly moisten a piece or part of the paper to make it easier to apply soft pleats. When wet-folding paper, make certain the paper dyes do not run or flake or get onto your fingers. You want to avoid leaving fingerprints all over your origami projects! Wet-folding can also be used on fabrics with the aid of spray-on fabric stiffener and a blow dryer.

Symbols

Symbols are used in origami to indicate a forth-coming action. In this book, you will usually see the symbol placed on the photograph immediately before the text instructs you to complete the action.

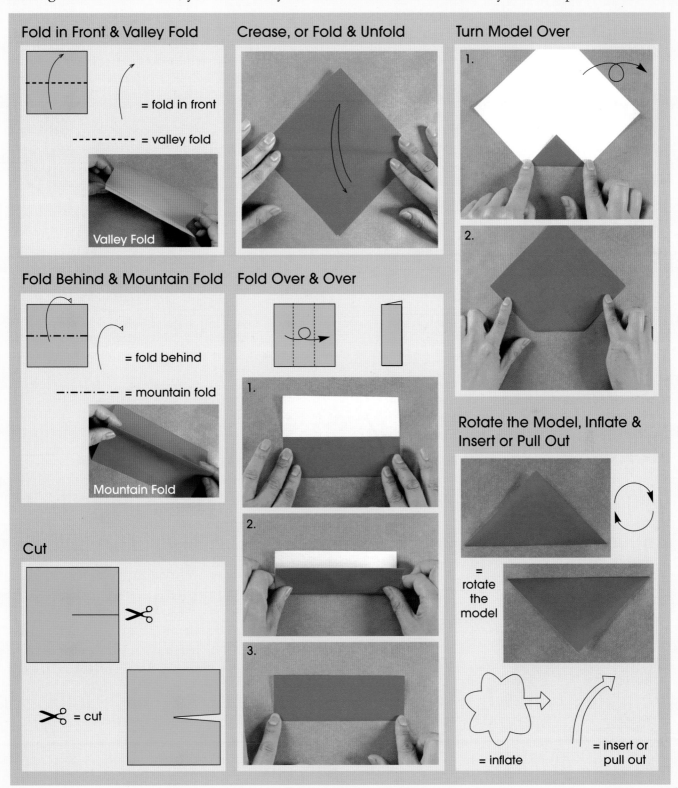

Fold in Front & Valley Fold

= fold in front

- - - - - - - = valley fold

Valley Fold

Fold Behind & Mountain Fold

= fold behind

—·—·—·— = mountain fold

Mountain Fold

Cut

✂ = cut

Crease, or Fold & Unfold

Fold Over & Over

1.

2.

3.

Turn Model Over

1.

2.

Rotate the Model, Inflate & Insert or Pull Out

= rotate the model

= inflate

= insert or pull out

Previous Position

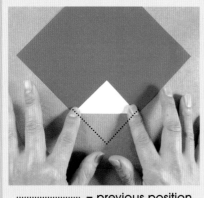

.... = previous position

Fold Over & Fold Back, or Pleat Fold

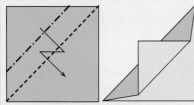

1.

2.

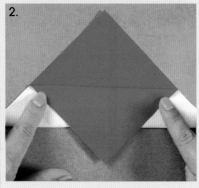

Press or Push In, Enlarge, Reduce & Place Finger Between Layers

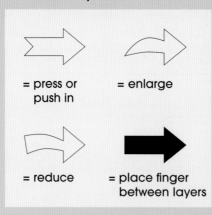

= press or push in

= enlarge

= reduce

= place finger between layers

Inside Reverse Fold

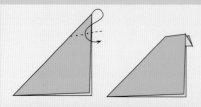

1. Crease the tip.

2. Open the model and collapse the tip to the inside.

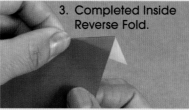

3. Completed Inside Reverse Fold.

Outside Reverse Fold

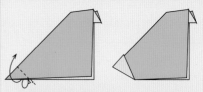

1. Crease the tip beyond the fold.

2. Crease the tip to line up with the fold.

3. Open the model.

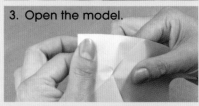

4. Reverse the fold to the outside.

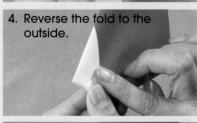

5. Pinch the tip and pull it away from the model to move the fold to the first crease line.

How do I fold origami paper?

Making a Crease

Lay the paper on a hard flat surface. Make the indicated fold by matching up the points and holding them with the index finger of the left hand. Slide the index finger of the right hand from the matched points to the opposite side of the paper and the center of the fold. (See Fig. 1) Move your index finger on the left hand from the matched points and position it to the left of the right-hand index finger. Slide it from the center of the fold outward to the left along the fold. (See Fig. 2) Hold the center of the fold with your left-hand index finger and slide the right-hand index finger from the center of the fold outward to the right of the fold. (See Fig. 3) This method should produce a sharp crease every time.

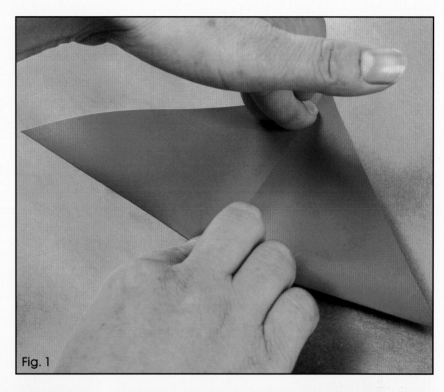

Fig. 1

Fig. 2

Fig. 3

When a flat surface is not available, you can also create a sharp crease by pinching the paper crease lightly between your thumbnail and index finger and moving along the edge of the fold. This method also comes in handy for relaxing an open crease or creating a light curl in the paper.

How do I make the basic folds and forms?

Basic Folds

Before learning a few common origami basic forms, practice simple convex and concave folding techniques to develop precision and crisp creasing.

Mountain & Valley Folds

Mountain and valley folds are also referred to as convex and concave folds. (See Fig. 4) The first fold—the convex, or mountain, fold (marked with a _._._._ line)—refers to folding down or away from you so that the crease faces toward you. The second fold—the concave, or valley, fold (marked with a _ _ _ _ line)—refers to folding up or toward you so that the crease faces away from you.

Accordion Folds

Accordion folds are also referred to as stair-step folds, zigzag folds, fan folds, and shell folds. These folds are simply consecutive convex and concave folds or pleats. (See Fig. 5) The first figure shows the accordion fold applied to a sheet of square paper and can be easily adapted to rectangular sheets. The middle figure shows the accordion fold adapted to a circular piece of doily paper and can be easily applied to ovals and half circles. The figure to the right shows the accordion fold applied to a sheet of square paper folded along the diagonal and can be easily applied to triangles. This figure has been slightly gathered at the bottom to demonstrate how applying accordion folds to the diagonal of a square sheet can easily turn a square sheet into a leaf or frond.

Fig. 4

Fig. 5

Basic, or Base, Forms

The following basic, or base, forms are the foundations for creating every origami project in this book. Once you have mastered these forms you will be able to use them as a starting point and add onto them with specific folds to create a particular figure.

Basic Form I: Ice Cream Base

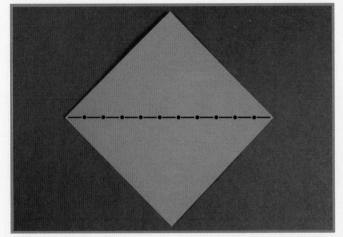

1. Begin with a square.

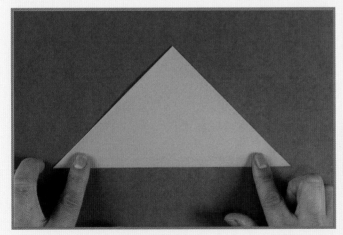

2. Fold in half diagonally (wrong side of paper is on the inside).

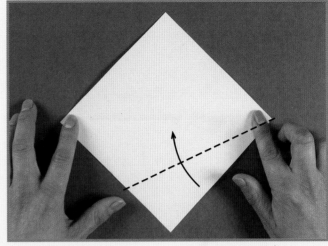

3. Unfold to show crease. Turn model over.

4. Fold top and bottom right sides to the horizontal midline.

5. Rotate model. Completed Ice Cream Base.

23

Basic Form II: Helmet Base

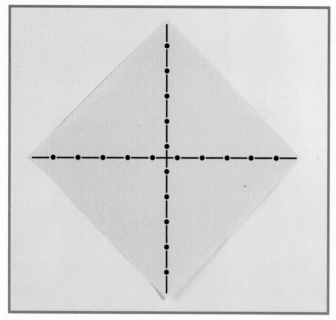

1. Begin with a square.

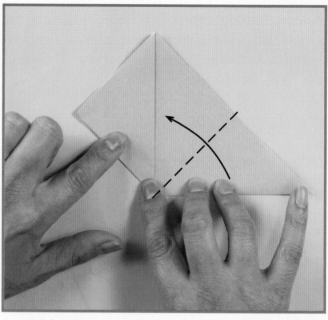

3. Fold left and right corners up along vertical midline to meet at top corner.

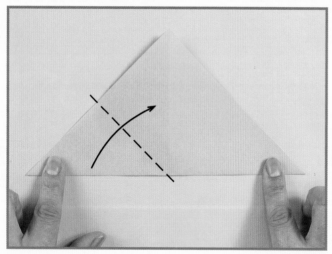

2. Fold and unfold in half diagonally in both directions (wrong side of paper is on the inside).

4. Completed Helmet Base.

Folding Hints

- Dedicate a time and place for origami as it requires a high level of concentration.

- Whenever possible, work on a hard, flat surface.

- Use a paper that is thin yet strong enough to withstand continuous folding without stretching.

- Work with precision and exactness, making straight folds and clean corners.

Basic Form III: Mat Base

1. Begin with a square. Fold in half (wrong side of paper is inside).

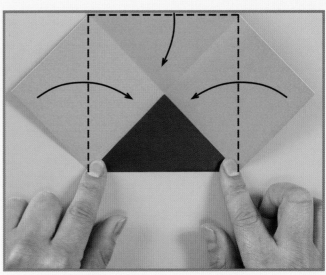

3. Unfold to show creases. Turn model over. Fold all corners to the center.

2. Unfold. Rotate and fold in half in other direction.

4. Completed Mat Base.

• Smooth all folds and creases with your thumbnail, a library or credit card, or a bone folder.

• Follow all steps in order. After each fold, position your model exactly as shown in the photograph.

• Be aware of the progression of the form—keep in mind the previous step and be prepared for the next.

• Study the form, practice folding, and use your imagination.

Basic Form IV: Twin Boat Base

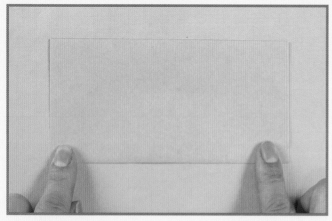

1. Begin with a square. Fold in half (right side of paper is inside).

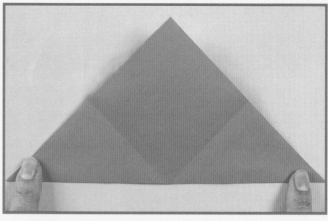

4. Unfold. Rotate and fold in half diagonally in other direction (wrong side of paper is inside).

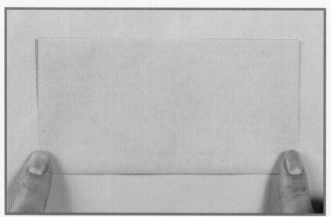

2. Unfold. Rotate and fold in half in other direction (right side of paper is inside).

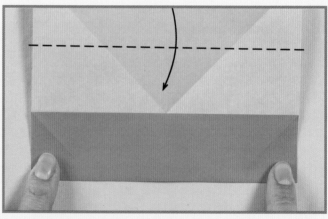

5. Unfold. Fold bottom edge to horizontal midline (wrong side of paper is inside).

3. Unfold. Fold in half diagonally (wrong side of paper is inside).

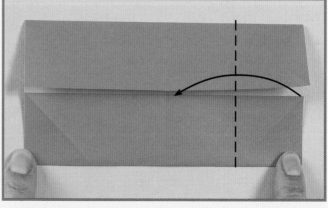

6. Fold top edge to horizontal midline (wrong side of paper is inside).

7. Rotate and fold bottom edge to horizontal midline.

9. Unfold last two folds. Fold the left corner up and to the right.

8. Fold top edge to horizontal midline.

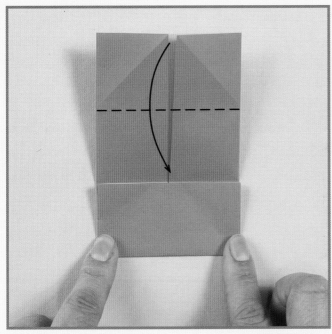

10. Unfold. Fold the right corner up and to the left.

11. Lift the bottom edge. Pull each corner up and pinch out.

12. Flatten this edge toward the center.

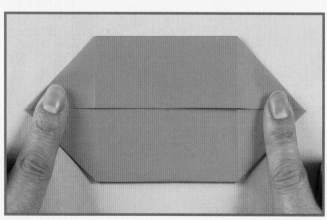

13. Repeat Steps 11–12 to fold the top edge. Completed Twin Boat Base.

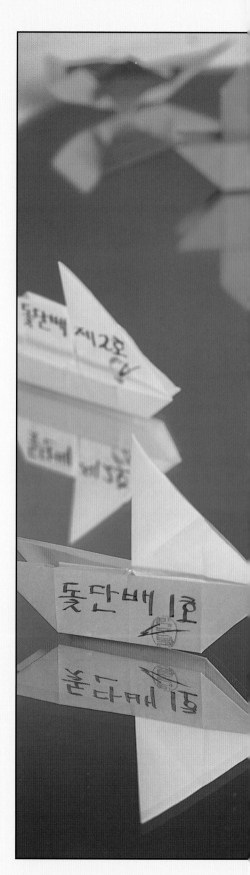

Basic Form V: Triangle Pocket Base

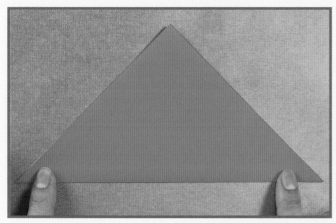

1. Begin with a square. Fold and unfold in half diagonally in both directions (wrong side of paper is inside).

2. Rotate and fold in half (right side of paper is inside).

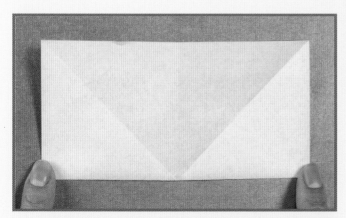

3. Unfold. Rotate and fold in half in other direction (right side of paper is inside).

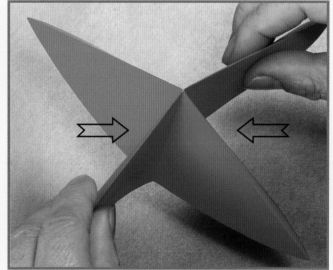

4. Unfold. Turn model over. Collapse two opposite sides to the center along the horizontal fold.

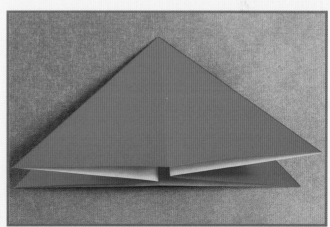

5. Flatten model. Completed Triangle Pocket Base.

1. Begin with a square. Fold in half (wrong side of paper is inside).

4. Unfold. Fold in half diagonally in other direction (right side of paper is inside).

2. Unfold. Rotate and fold in half in other direction.

5. Unfold. Turn model over.

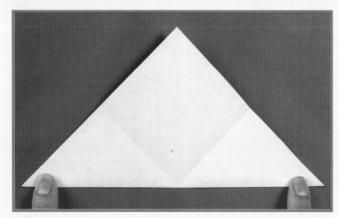

3. Unfold. Turn model over. Fold in half diagonally (right side of paper is inside).

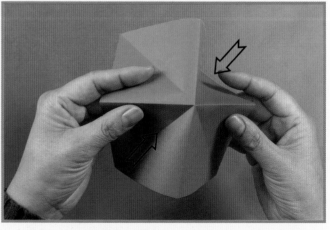

6. Fold two opposite side corners to meet at center.

7. Flatten model. Completed Square Base.

Benefits of Origami

• Because origami requires mental discipline, it promotes clear thinking and builds character.

• Origami has proven useful for small muscle development—especially for small children and people involved in rehabilitative physical therapy.

• This paper art form links you to a diverse group of people all over the world as there are numerous origami clubs and associations that can be found locally, nationally, and internationally via the internet.

• Origami can be a fairly inexpensive hobby. You can use almost any type of paper that will not stretch after folding it. Do not underestimate the value of recycling. Save your paper scraps and ask your friends to save their scraps, too. If you want to use the more expensive origami papers, you should first use a "practice" piece of paper to work up the model. When you are certain of how to arrive at the completed form, make the folds again—this time using your fine origami paper.

Basic Form VII: Crane Base

1. Begin with the Square Base.

2. With opening at the bottom, fold bottom left side of upper flap to vertical midline.

3. Fold bottom right side of upper flap to vertical midline.

5. Unfold last three folds.

4. Rotate and fold folded corner of Square Base up to the center.

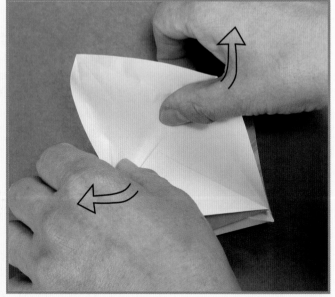

6. Rotate model and begin to form the upper wing by opening the upper flap at the bottom point, pulling it up as far as possible.

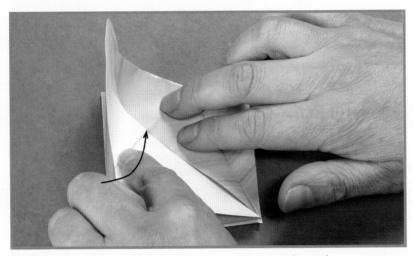

7. Press at left and right flap corners so the edges meet at the midline.

8. This will form a diamond. Turn the model over. Repeat Steps 2–7.

9. Completed Crane Base.

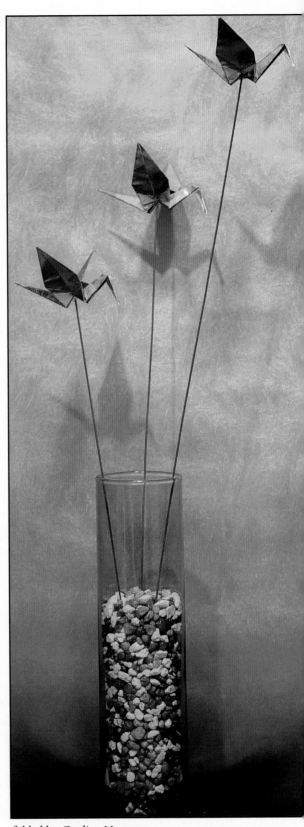

folded by Geoline Havener

Basic Form VIII: Fish Base

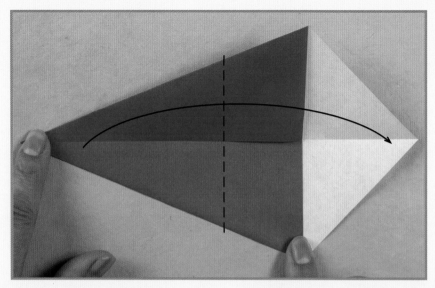

1. Begin with the Ice Cream Base.

2. Rotate model and fold in half, bringing bottom corner to meet top corner.

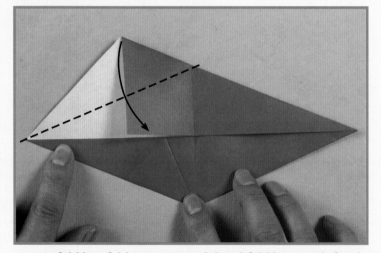

3. Unfold last fold. Rotate model and fold bottom left side to horizontal midline.

4. Rotate model and fold bottom right side to horizontal midline.

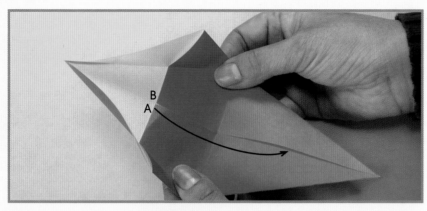

5. Unfold the last two folds.

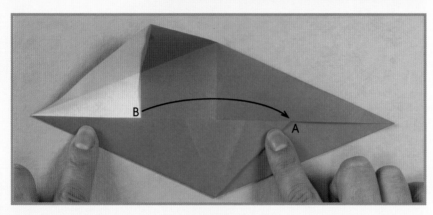

6. Lift corner A and then pull it downward so the side point moves toward the horizontal midline.

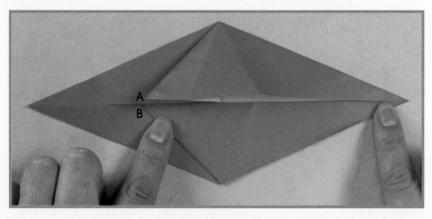

7. Rotate model. Lift corner B and then pull it downward so the side point moves toward the horizontal midline.

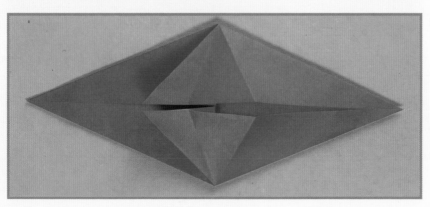

8. Completed Fish Base.

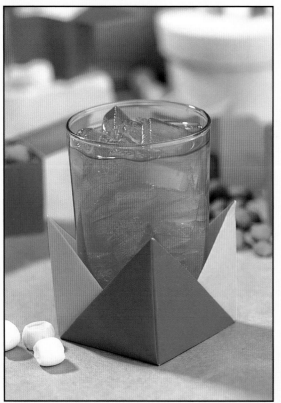

Section 2: basic techniques

1
technique

What you need to get started:

Craft glue stick
Origami papers, 3" square:
  blue (2), green (2), red (2),
  yellow (2)

How can I use a simple model?

This project is actually the result of combining eight easy-to-make models into one. The colors shown here are the traditional colors of Korea. You can choose any color combination you desire to go with the theme of a tea party or to match a room's decor.

Coaster

Here's how:

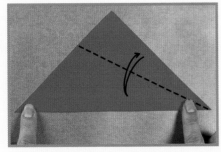

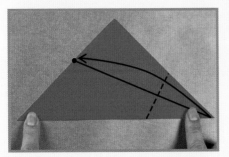

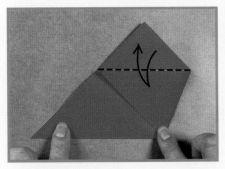

1. Begin with a square. Fold in half diagonally. Crease along dashed line.

2. Fold right corner to meet opposite point of crease.

3. Crease top-upper corner along dashed line.

4. Tuck top-upper corner into top triangle.

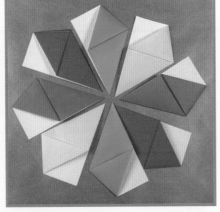

5. Repeat Steps 1–4 to make two models of each color.

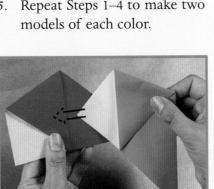

6. Insert top corner of one model into bottom of top triangle of another model.

7. Secure the assembly at its center with the thumb of the left hand.

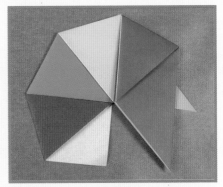

Note: To help secure the assembly, apply glue to inside-top corner before inserting it into the triangle of the other model.

8. Repeat Steps 6–7, alternating colors, until you have half of the assembly.

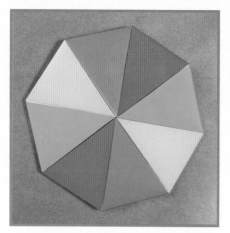

9. Repeat Steps 6–7 for second half. Assemble the two halves to create a combined model.

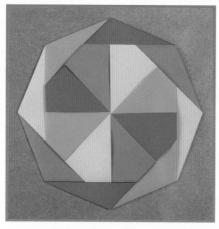

12. Completed Coaster.

Tips

Cut a 6"-square piece of origami paper in half, then in half again to get four 3"-square pieces of paper.

Use 1"- or 2"-square pieces of paper to make a smaller completed model and use it for a bookmark.

Tuck a note or a small photo into the folds and the coaster becomes a chic gift card.

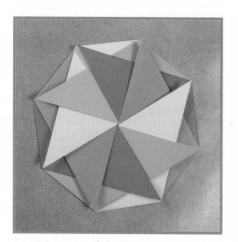

10. Turn model over.

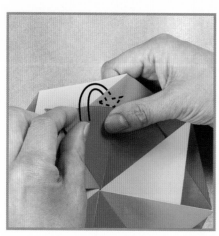

11. Tuck corner of each color under the fold that lies immediately below it.

Use a combination of printed and solid papers to achieve the clean black-and-white look shown above.

How can I make two projects from the same basic model?

The first five steps for making each of these models are exactly the same. Learn how a few simple variations make the difference in the final outcome.

What you need to get started:

Origami papers, 6" square:
  blue (2)

Paper Cup

Here's how:

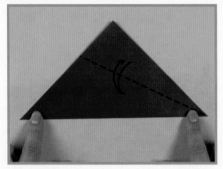

1. Begin with a square. Fold in half diagonally. Crease along dashed line.

2. Fold right corner to meet opposite point of crease.

3. Crease top-upper corner along dashed line.

4. Fold left corner to meet opposite point.

5. Tuck top-upper corner into top triangle.

Note: The model will look like this after making the tuck.

6. Turn model over. Rotate and fold top corner toward center.

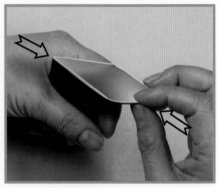

7. Open model by pushing in on both sides.

8. Completed Paper Cup.

Snack Cup

Here's how:

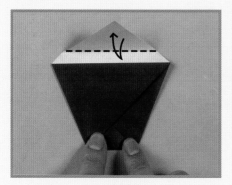

1. Refer to Paper Cup on page 42. Complete Steps 1–5. Crease top corner along dashed line.

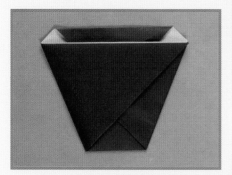

2. Tuck top corner inside cup.

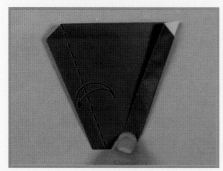

3. Turn model over. Crease left and right sides along the dashed lines.

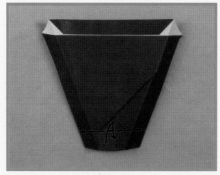

4. Turn model over.

5. Crease the bottom along the dashed line.

6. Open model by flattening left, right, and bottom sides from the inside.

7. Pinch each bottom corner and fold toward the center for a flat bottom.

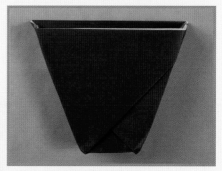

8. Completed Snack Cup.

Tips

You can use either of these cups to hold actual food items such as popcorn, carrot sticks, potato chips, dried fruit mix, french fries, etc.

Use oil paper or waxed paper to make a cup that will hold liquid or wet food.

If you would like to place larger or pointed items such as pencils and scissors in your cup, you can use a larger square in a card stock or other heavier-weight paper.

What you need to get started:

Origami paper, 4" square: magenta/pink diagonally striped

How do I make a heart shape?

This familiar shape is perfect for dressing up love notes and small tokens of affection. You can use this model to create your own custom-made valentines, name tags for a bridal shower, or place cards for a romantic dinner.

Paper Heart

Here's how:

1. Begin with a square. Fold in half (wrong side of the paper is inside).

2. Unfold. Rotate and fold in half in other direction (wrong side of paper is inside).

3. Unfold. Fold bottom edge to the horizontal midline (wrong side of paper is inside).

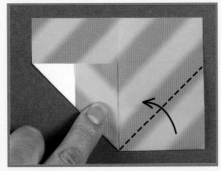

4. Turn model over. Fold bottom-left corner to vertical midline.

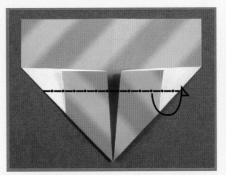

5. Fold bottom-right corner to vertical midline.

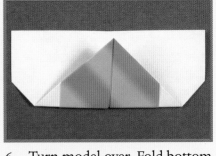

6. Turn model over. Fold bottom corner to top edge.

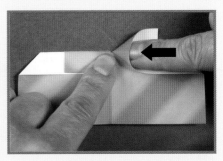

7. Turn model over. Rotate and place your index finger between layers on the right side as indicated.

8. Press to flatten.

Tips

Make a four-leaf clover for St. Patrick's Day, using four Paper Hearts from green origami paper. Glue them together so that the points touch. Similarly, make a daisy by using four Paper Hearts from white paper and coloring a yellow dot in the center.

Create a bright-colored paper crown by omitting Steps 13–14 on page 46 and gluing eight or more models together in a circle.

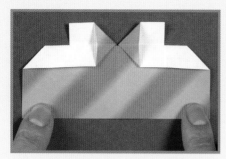

9. Repeat Steps 7–8 for left side.

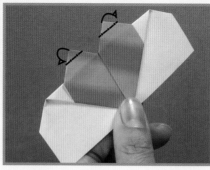

11. Repeat Step 10 for top-right corner of heart.

13. Turn model over. Fold each side to the back along the dashed lines.

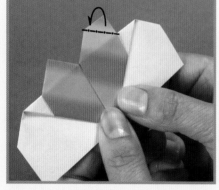

10. Turn model over. Fold top-left corner of heart to back.

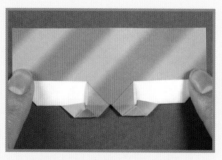

12. Turn model over. Fold each corner on heart along the dashed lines.

14. Completed Paper Heart.

Tips

Slip the heart over the top edge of a handwritten note.

Give your heart wings. Pleat-fold a rectangle of matching paper and secure it onto the back side of the heart.

Make an easel for your heart so it can stand.

Layer two hearts of different sizes.

How do I turn a model inside out?

technique

For this project, you will reverse the final fold so the model stands on its own. To achieve the two-toned effect, you will make two duplicate models—one from each color—and set one within the other.

What you need to get started:

Origami papers, 6" square: magenta, pink

Cup Holder

Here's how:

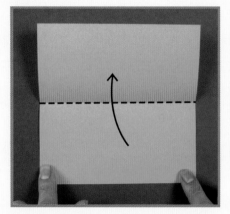

1. Begin with a square. Fold in half (right side of the paper is inside).

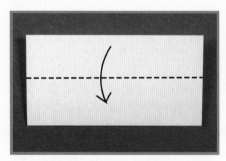

2. Fold top-upper edge along dashed line to fold.

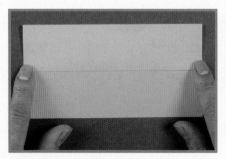

Note: The model will look like this after making the fold.

3. Turn model over. Crease along dashed line.

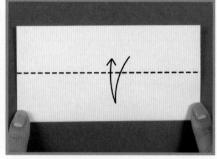

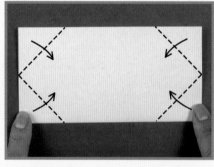

4. Fold all corners along dashed lines to horizontal midline.

Note: For ease in working, rotate the model and make the folds at one end; then repeat for remaining end.

5. Fold left side up and to the right along dashed line.

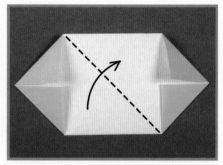

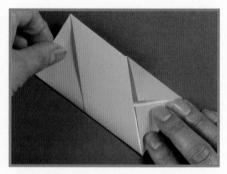

Note: The model will look like this after making the fold.

6. Unfold last fold. Fold right side up and to the left along the dashed line.

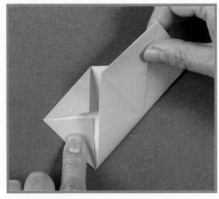

Note: The model will look like this after making the fold.

7. Unfold the last fold to show the creases.

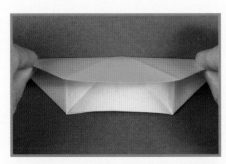

8. Fold model in half along horizontal midline (wrong side is inside).

9. Turn the model upright. Insert your thumbs between the layers and pull edges outward, turning the model inside out and creating a flat bottom.

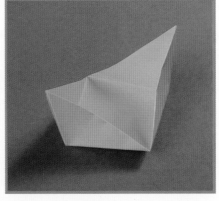

10. Repeat Steps 1–9 to make a second model.

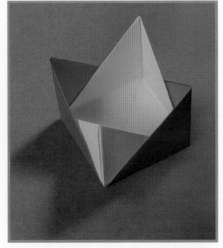

11. Set one model within the other. Completed Cup Holder.

Tip

The next time you throw a garden party, place a flower arrangement on the cocktail table and make cup holders to match. Set out a marking pen so each guest can write their name on their cup holder to keep track of which drink belongs to whom.

5
technique

What you need
to get started:

Origami paper, 6" square:
magenta

By beginning with one of the basic forms, you can easily create this small container, which serves as a wonderful party accessory for holding individual portions of nuts and candies.

50

Candy Cup

Here's how:

1. Refer to Basic Form III: Mat Base on page 25. Begin with a Mat Base.

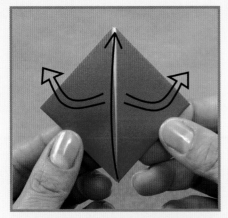

2. Refer to Basic Form VI: Square Base on page 30. Fold Mat Base as if it were a simple square to change the form and produce the Square Base.

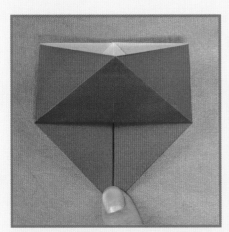

3. Push bottom-upper point to top of model and press to flatten. Turn model over and repeat.

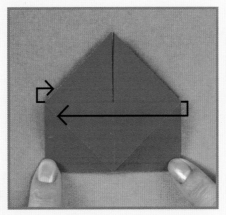

4. Rotate the model. Fold the right-upper layer to the left side and the left-lower layer to the right side.

Note: The model will look like this after making the folds.

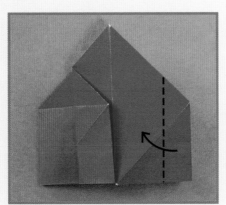

5. Fold each side edge to center along dashed lines. Turn model over and repeat.

6. Fold top-upper corner down to bottom of model. Turn model over and repeat.

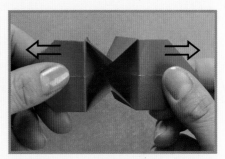

7. Open model by pulling the resulting flaps outward.

8. Completed Candy Cup.

Note: The model is shown as viewed from the top.

6
technique

What you need to get started:

Decorative-edged scissors:
  scallop
Paper place mat, 13½" x 9½":
  red / white plaid
Rotary trimmer

There are so many different designs available for paper products today, that this project could be used for almost any dinner or party setting. For example, a place mat with a floral design would set the tone for an afternoon tea, while one with a harvest design would be just right for Thanksgiving.

Utensil Holder

Developed by Soonboke Smith

Here's how:

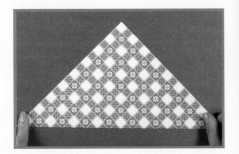

1. Using a rotary trimmer, trim place mat into a 9" square. Fold in half diagonally (wrong side of paper is inside).

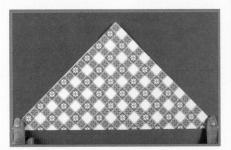

2. Unfold. Fold in half diagonally in other direction (wrong side of paper is inside).

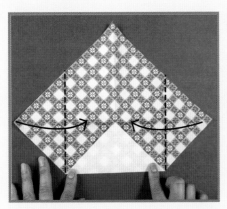

3. Unfold to show creases. Fold left, right, and bottom corners to center.

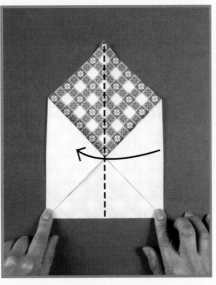

4. Fold model in half along dashed line.

5. Using a pair of decorative-edged scissors, trim along top angled edge.

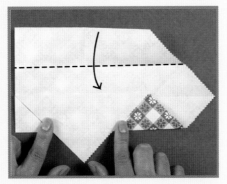

6. Unfold last fold. Turn model over and fold left and right sides to center along the dashed lines.

Note: The model will look like this after making the folds. The left and right sides will be overlapping slightly.

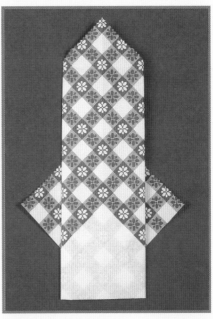

7. Turn model over. Completed Utensil Holder.

Tip

Try folding this project from a square cloth napkin. Choose a napkin that is double-sided—either with two different solid colors or with a solid color on one side and a print on the other side.

Note: Do not cut or trim napkin.

7
technique

What you need to get started:

Beads for flower
  centers
Craft glue stick
Letterhead, 6" square:
  terra-cotta for pot
Mat board, 6" square:
  white
Mulberry papers,
  ¾" square: peach/ecru
  for petals (64)
Origami papers, ¾"
  square: dark green
  for leaves (10)
White tacky glue

How can I use the Ice Cream Base form?

This lovely accent piece can be made in one afternoon. The pot, flowers, and leaves require simple folding, a bit of glue, and a square piece of mat board on which to arrange them. You can purchase a square shadow-box frame to display your work and have it hanging on your sitting room wall the very same evening.

Flowerpot

Here's how:

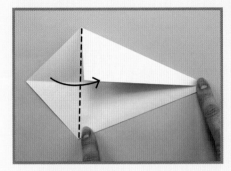

1. Refer to Basic Form I: Ice Cream Base on page 23. Begin with an Ice Cream Base.

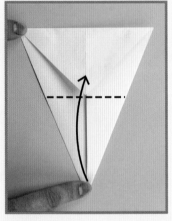

2. Rotate model. Fold top corner down toward center.

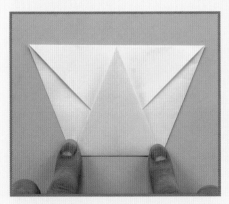

3. Fold bottom corner up to meet top folded edge.

4. Turn model over. Completed Flowerpot.

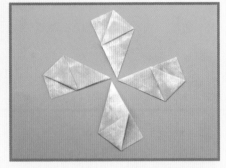

5. Refer to Coaster on page 39. Complete Steps 1–4 to make four models.

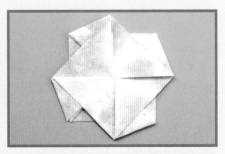

6. Glue two petals together for half of the assembly.

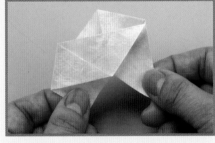

7. Repeat Step 6 for second half. Assemble the two halves to create a combined model.

8. Turn model over. Completed Flower. Glue beads on center.

9. Pleat-fold along the diagonal.

10. Fold corners to back.

11. Fold edges to back, rounding the shape. Completed Leaf.

12. Repeat Steps 5–11 to make 16 flowers and 10 leaves.

13. Glue onto mat board as desired.

Section 3: beyond the basics

1 project

How do I make a box that is shaped like a bird?

What you need to get started:

Origami paper, 6" square: gray

Turn this lovely swan, which begins with the Ice Cream Base, into a box by pushing the tail toward the inside of the model. By resting on its wings, it is able to stand upright.

58

Swan Box

Here's how:

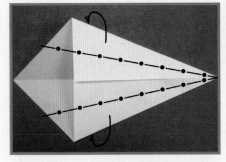

1. Refer to Basic Form I: Ice Cream Base on page 23. Begin with an Ice Cream Base.

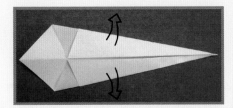

2. Turn model over. Fold top and bottom corners to horizontal midline.

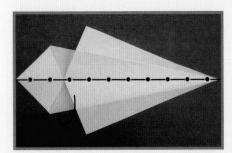

3. Pull flaps out from behind. Fold in half (to the back) along horizontal midline.

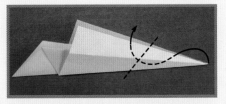

4. Crease along dashed line.

5. Reverse-fold by opening the model and collapsing the tip to the inside, keeping the center fold at the center.

Note: The model will look like this after making the folds.

6. Fold along dashed line.

7. Tuck corner under top wing.

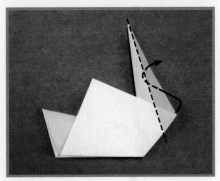

8. Crease upper and lower flaps along dashed line.

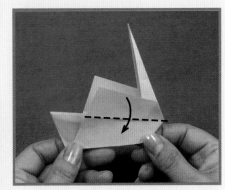

9. Reverse-fold by opening each flap and collapsing each tip to the inside.

10. Fold each wing downward so top edge meets bottom fold.

12. Reverse-fold by opening the neck and collapsing the tip to the inside. Push the tail toward the inside of the model.

11. Crease neck along dashed line.

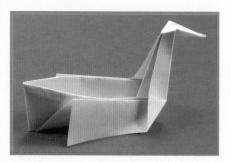

13. Completed Swan Box.

Tips

You can accordion-fold a piece of blue paper along the diagonal to serve as a "lake" for your swan.

This box makes a charming decorative container for a wedding celebration.

Make a swan for each guest who will be attending the wedding ceremony. Fill each box with rice. Pass them out so guests can shower the newly married couple as they leave the altar.

Set two swans on the head table at a wedding luncheon— one for the bride and one for the groom. The happy couple can use the swans as a means to deliver a note or token of love for one another.

At a wedding reception, the swans can be set on guest tables to hold mints, confetti, or rose petals.

Use the Swan Box as a favor cup to accent a child's birthday party. This is especially nice if the party is held at a park or at the zoo where the guests have been able to see real swans.

For more-casual use, this box can be placed on your coffee table to hold tea bags or sugar cubes. You could even use it as a teaspoon rest if you are willing to throw it away after use.

How do I make a triangular box?

Made up of three separate interlocking pieces, this tiny box is like a three-dimensional puzzle. Place a surprise inside and watch the wonder in the eyes of the one who discovers the secret to opening it.

What you need to get started:

Origami papers, 3" square: blue, green, red

61

Tricolor Gift Box

Here's how:

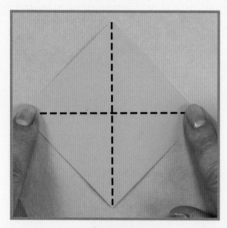

1. Begin with a square.

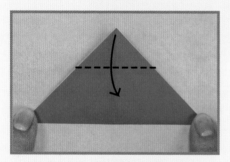

2. Fold in half diagonally in both directions (wrong side of the paper is inside).

3. Fold top-upper corner down to bottom, creating a flap.

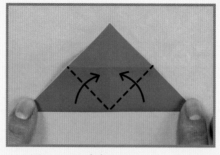

4. Turn model over.

5. Fold left and right corners along dashed lines to meet at top corner.

6. Repeat Steps 1–5 with two contrasting colored pieces of paper to make three models.

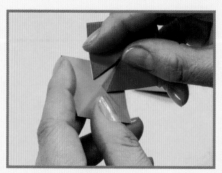

7. Position the points of one model opposite the flap of another model.

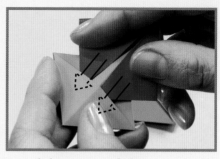

8. Slide points of the one model under the flap of the other.

Note: The model will look like this after assembling the two pieces.

9. Repeat Steps 7–8, sliding points of remaining model under flap of second model.

10. Pull points of first model outward, separating them.

11. Bring corner of third model toward center of first model.

12. Tuck points of first model under flap of third model.

13. Completed Tricolor Gift Box.

Tips

For a New Year's Eve party, make this box from metallic paper and fill it with confetti. At the stroke of midnight, party guests can open the box and throw their confetti.

At Christmas time, make the box from seasonal wrapping paper. Insert tiny gifts such as candy kisses, coins, and folded dollar bills. String a fine metallic cord through the paper at one point of the box and hang it as an ornament on the Christmas tree.

Add a tassel at the bottom of the box and a fine metallic cord at the top. Hang the ornament from cupboard drawer pulls and doorknobs.

folded by Kim Unju

Use ½"- to 1"-square pieces of paper to make several tiny triangular boxes. Make some boxes from clear plastic or vellum and place rolled up multicolored strips of paper that have handwritten notes on them inside these transparent boxes. Place the tiny boxes inside another container such as a decorative glass bottle with a cork or a posh gift box like those shown in the photo above.

3 project

What you need to get started:

Craft glue stick
Origami papers, 6" square:
  glossy rainbow check (4)
Photo of choice, 4½" square

How do I make a simple frame?

This simple picture frame, made up of four identical pieces, is also very versatile. You can turn the frame over and use the back side for the front. If you would like a white mat for your picture, simply skip Steps 4–7 and fold the center-upper flap to the back.

Picture Frame

Here's how:

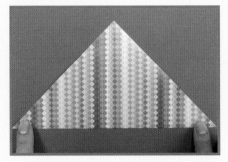

1. Begin with a square. Fold in half diagonally in both directions (wrong side of paper is inside).

Note: After making the second fold, the rainbow stripes should be running horizontally.

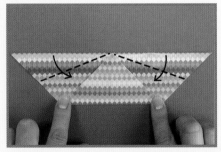

2. Rotate model. Fold bottom corner up to top edge.

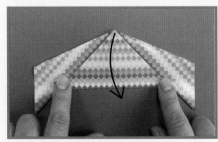

3. Fold left and right corners downward so top edges meet left and right edges of folded-up bottom corner.

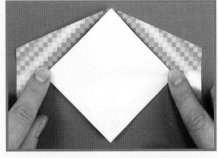

4. Unfold center-upper flap.

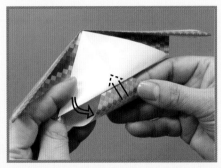

5. Tuck this flap inside the model.

6. Unfold remaining center flap and tuck it inside the model.

7. Repeat Steps 1–6 to make four models.

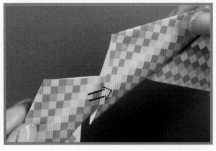

8. Apply glue to the right point of one model and slide it inside the left point of another model.

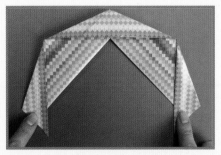

Note: The model will look like this after assembling the two pieces.

9. Repeat Step 8, gluing and sliding the remaining point inside the opposite point of the next model, until you have assembled a square.

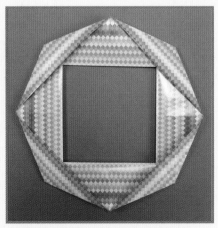

10. Completed Picture Frame.

11. Secure photo onto back of frame with glue.

4
project

What you need to get started:

Craft scissors
Paper doily, 10" diameter:
   round, white

How can I use a round piece of paper?

You will be pleasantly surprised at the ease with which you are able to accomplish this delicate figure of a dove. The lacey edge on the doily creates the illusion of feathers and lends the entire model a light and airy quality.

Dove

Here's how:

1. Begin with a circle.

2. Cut circle in half.

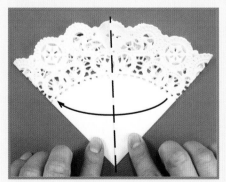

3. Fold left and right corners up to top edge.

4. Fold in half so folded corners are inside model.

5. Cut model as indicated.

6. Rotate model so last fold is the top edge and lace edges are to the right. Fold bottom-upper corner up.

7. Fold bottom-lower corner to the back and up.

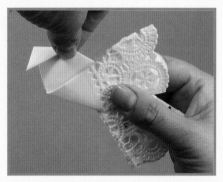

8. Crease neck along dashed line.

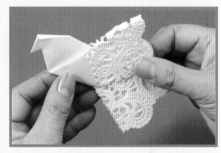

9. Reverse-fold by opening the neck and collapsing the tip to the inside.

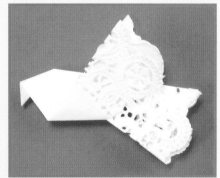

10. Completed Dove.

67

How can I build on the Mat Base form?

What you need to get started:

Craft glue stick
Medium-weight papers,
   10" square: purple (2)

This project repeats the actions used in creating the Mat Base two times to yield a dimensional model. It is made from medium-weight paper for stability. You can make this pen holder three or four times larger, fill it with goodies, and use it for a gift basket.

Pen Holder

Here's how:

1. Refer to Basic Form III: Mat Base on page 25. Begin with a Mat Base.

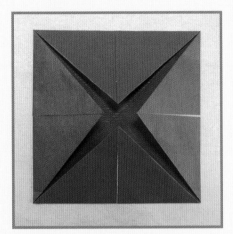

2. Turn model over. Fold each corner to center.

3. Turn model over. Fold each corner to center.

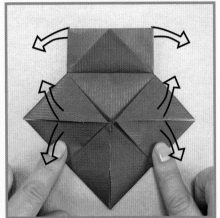

4. Turn model over. Push bottom-upper point of one diamond to top of model and pull inside edges to outside. Press to flatten.

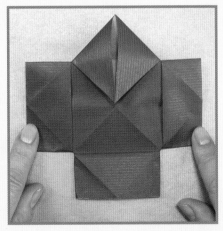

5. Rotate model and repeat Step 4 (without turning model over). Repeat again for three straight sides.

6. Repeat Steps 1–5 to make two models.

7. Fold the straight sides of each model back toward the center. Position the models so their insides are facing each other.

8. Apply glue to straight sides of one model. Slide these sides into the matching sides of the facing model.

9. Completed Pen Holder

6
project

What you need to get started:

Craft glue stick
Medium-weight papers,
  7" square: purple (2)

How do I make matching pieces?

There are several figures in origami that will go together in a setting, such as a horse and rider or a hen and its chick. This peewee chair and table are certain to prove irresistible to the hands and imaginations of children and the young at heart.

Chair

Here's how:

1. Refer to Pen Holder on page 69. Complete Steps 1–4.

Refer to Pen Holder on page 69.

> **Tip**
> Insert a folded piece of paper into the top edge of the chair back to cover the gap.

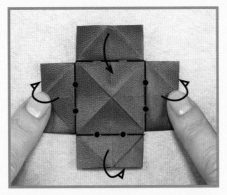

2. Rotate model and repeat previous action for each side.

3. Fold one side forward and three sides backward so model will stand. Completed Chair.

Table

Here's how:

1. Begin with a square. Fold in half in both directions (wrong side of paper is inside). Unfold to show creases.

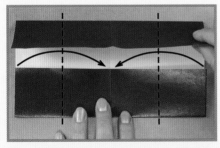

2. Fold top and bottom edges to the horizontal midline (wrong side of paper is inside).

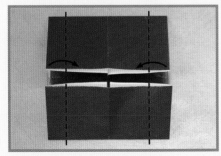

3. Rotate model. Repeat Step 2.

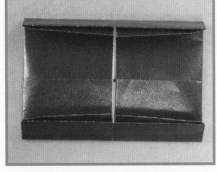

4. Rotate model. Fold top and bottom edges one third of the distance to the horizontal midline.

5. Unfold last two folds. Fold each corner to meet creases.

6. Unfold the corners. Place your index finger between layers at the bottom right corner as indicated and press to flatten. Repeat for each corner.

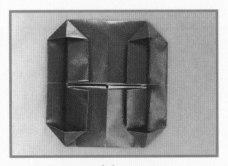

7. Rotate model.

8. Fold two side flaps upward.

9. Turn model over so table stands. Completed Table.

7 project

What you need to get started:

Origami papers, 6" square:
bright green for sailboat,
patterned for pinwheel

How can I use the Twin Boat Base form?

Here you will learn how to make two fanciful models from the same basic form. You will note that both figures begin with the Mat Base to ensure clean edges, then progress to the Twin Boat Base to create the foundation for the completed model.

Pinwheel

Here's how:

1. Refer to Basic Form III: Mat Base on page 25. Begin with a Mat Base.

2. Refer to Basic Form IV: Twin Boat Base on page 26. Fold Mat Base as if it were a simple square to produce the Twin Boat Base.

Tips

Make your pinwheel from paper colors and patterns that coordinate with your office accessories. Use the pinwheel to decorate a bookmark, a folder, or an envelope.

Make several pinwheels and use them for party decorations and favors. For each, paint a ¼"-diameter wooden dowel with colors to match your pinwheel. Insert a push pin through the center of the pinwheel. Push the pin into the upper edge of the painted wooden dowel.

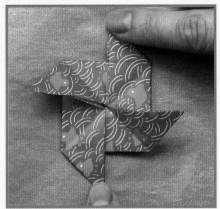

3. Fold top-right flap up and to the right along vertical midline. Fold bottom-right flap down and to the left.

4. Completed Pinwheel.

Sailboat

Here's how:

1. Refer to Basic Form III: Mat Base on page 25. Begin with a Mat Base.

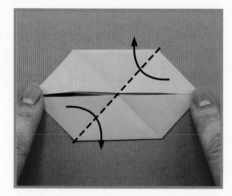

2. Refer to Basic Form IV: Twin Boat Base on page 26. Fold Mat Base as if it were a simple square to produce the Twin Boat Base.

3. Lift each flap slightly. Hold the top-right flap with your right-hand thumb and index finger. Hold the bottom-left flap with your left-hand thumb and index finger. Fold top-right flap over and to the right so it is against the body of the model.

4. Fold top-right flap and body of the model as one diagonally to the back so that the point meets the point of the bottom-left flap.

5. Rotate so these two flaps make up the bottom edge of the model.

6. Completed Sailboat.

How can I use the Triangle Pocket Base form?

Unleash the part of you that loves to build things! Origami just may be the medium for expression that your inner architect has been waiting for. In this project, you will use a letter-sized piece of paper and one of the basic forms to yield a small structure with uniform peaks and angles.

What you need to get started:

Medium-weight paper, 8½" x 11": brick pattern
Origami paper, ½" strips: brown
Rotary trimmer

Barn

Here's how:

1. Trim paper into a 8½" square. Set aside the remaining paper strip for later use.

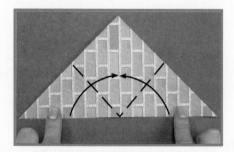

2. Refer to Basic Form V: Triangle Pocket Base on page 29. Begin with a Triangle Pocket Base made from large square.

3. Fold left- and right-upper corners along vertical midline to meet at top corner.

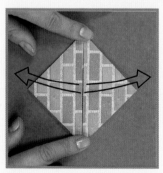

4. Turn model over and repeat Step 3.

5. Push top-upper point of each triangle to the bottom of model and pull inside edges to outside. Press to flatten.

6. Turn model over. Repeat Step 5.

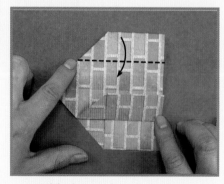

7. Fold the right-upper layer to the left side and the left-lower layer to the right side. Fold top- and bottom-upper flaps to horizontal midline. Rotate the model.

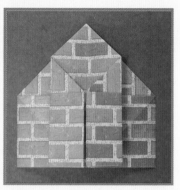

Note: The model will look like this after making the folds.

8. Turn model over. Repeat Step 7.

9. Fold the right-upper layer to the left side and the left-lower layer to the right side.

Note: The model will look like this after making the folds.

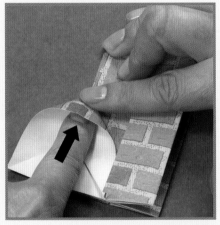

10. Place your index finger between flaps on the bottom-left side as indicated and press to flatten. Repeat for the bottom-right side.

11. Fold bottom-upper corner toward center to make center peak of barn.

12. From one end of remaining paper strip, cut a 1¾" square. Fold in half diagonally in both directions to form a triangle. Glue onto center peak of barn.

13. From remaining paper strip, cut two 2½" squares. Repeat Steps 2–6 for each square. Slide one resulting model onto each side edge of exhisting model. Glue to secure placement.

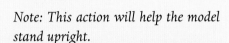

14. Pull out inner flaps on large model.

Note: This action will help the model stand upright.

15. Completed Barn.

16. Fashion a door bolt and brackets from small strips of brown origami paper. Glue onto barn doors.

Tips

Use a paper with a stone pattern to transform this model into a church or cathedral. You could make tiny doves to sit at its peaks. (Refer to Dove on page 67.) This would make a nice table decoration at your next church social.

Create a crèche for a nativity scene, using a paper with a wood plank pattern. Refer to other origami books for animal and human figures to complete the rest of the scene.

Make several models in different colors and sizes to create a town.

9 project

What you need to get started:

Ballpoint pen for curling petals

Floral tape: green

Floral wire: green

Marking pen, round tip: brown

Origami paper, 6" square: orange/yellow

Silk flower pistil and stamens

White tacky glue

How can I use the Square Base form?

This basic form will blossom into a beautiful garden flower right before your eyes. It looks so real that it will likely fool the bees.

Lily

Developed by Soonboke Smith

Here's how:

1. Refer to Basic Form VI: Square Base on page 30. Begin with a Square Base.

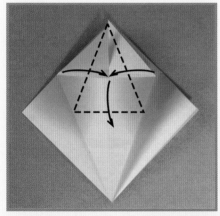

2. With opening at the top of the model, fold left-upper corner to vertical midline. Unfold.

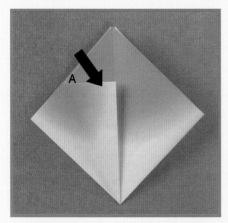

3. Place your index finger between layers of folded left-upper corner and move point A over to right side of model. Press to flatten.

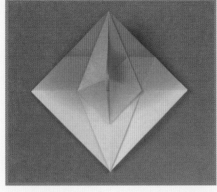

4. Crease along dashed lines. Push left and right points of resulting triangle to center of model and press to flatten.

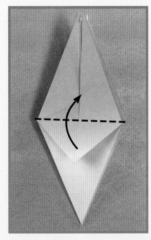

5. Turn model over and repeat Steps 2–4 for each side corner.

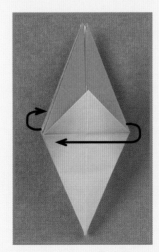

6. Fold bottom flap up. Repeat for each side.

7. Fold the right-upper layer to the left side and the left-lower layer to the right side.

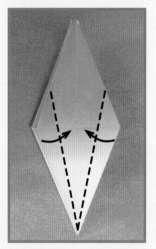

Note: The model will look like this after making the folds.

8. Fold left- and right-upper corners to vertical midline.

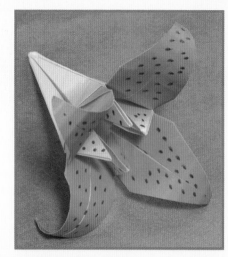

13. Insert one end of floral wire into the bottom of the lily. Wrap floral tape around the bottom point of the lily and continue wrapping downward around floral wire.

14. Apply a small amount of glue onto stem end of each silk flower pistil and stamen. Insert glued end into center of lily. Allow glue to dry.

9. Turn model over and repeat for each side.

12. Completed Lily.

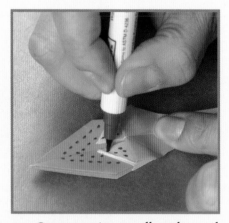

10. One at a time, pull each petal downward and dot over the surface, using marking pen.

11. Open flower by pulling petals downward and curling them under, using the shaft of a ballpoint pen.

Tip

Apply a thin even coat of clear nail polish over the flower's petals to make them shine.

How can I use the Crane Base form?

From this basic form comes one of the most recognizable origami figures—the crane. A symbol of hope and good wishes, the crane is often given at awards ceremonies or commencement exercises.

What you need to get started:

Origami paper, 6" square: orange/yellow

Soonboke's Crane

Developed by Soonboke Smith

Here's how:

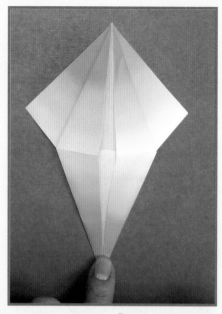

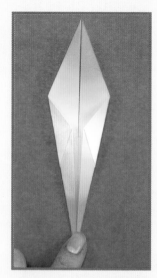

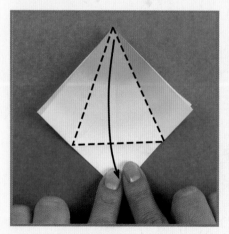

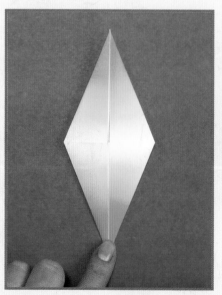

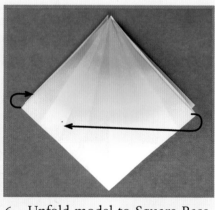

1. Refer to Basic Form VI: Square Base on page 30. Begin with a Square Base.

2. With opening at the top of the model, fold and unfold along dashed lines.

3. Open upper flap at the top point, pulling it down as far as possible. Press at left- and right-center corners so edges meet at the vertical midline. This will form a diamond.

4. Turn the model over. Repeat Steps 2–3.

Note: Refer to Basic Form VII: Crane Base on page 31. This is the Crane Base form.

5. Rotate model so opening is at the bottom. Fold left- and right-upper corners to vertical midline. Turn model over and repeat.

6. Unfold model to Square Base. Fold the right-upper layer to the left side and the left-lower layer to the right side.

Note: The model will look like this after making the folds. The creases will show on the wings of the completed crane for added dimension.

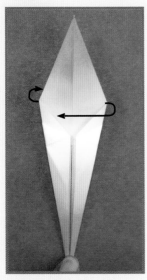

7. Repeat Steps 2–5.

8. Fold the right-upper layer to the left side and the left-lower layer to the right side.

9. Fold bottom-upper point up to top point. Turn model over and repeat.

10. Fold the right-upper layer to the left side and the left-lower layer to the right side.

11. Pull "tail" point outward and press to fold in place.

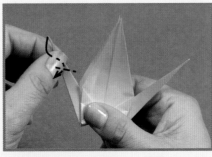

12. Pull "neck" point outward and press to fold in place.

13. Crease neck along dashed line.

14. Reverse-fold by opening the neck and collapsing the tip to the inside.

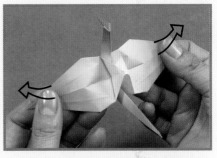

15. Pull the wings in opposite directions until the "back" begins to flatten somewhat.

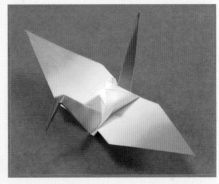

16. Completed Soonboke's Crane.

How do I make
an animated model?

What you need
to get started:

Origami paper, 6" square:
glossy rainbow check

This dainty crane is also capable of motion. By pulling on its tail, you can flap its wings. Small children will be mesmerized by the show of movement and color.

Flapping Crane

Here's how:

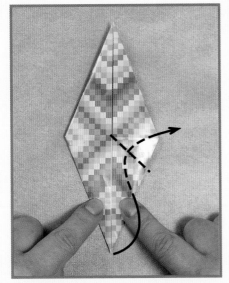

1. Refer to Basic Form VII: Crane Base on page 31. Begin with a Crane Base.

2. Rotate model so opening is at the bottom. Crease along the dashed line and reverse-fold by opening flap and collapsing the tip to the inside.

3. Crease along the dashed line and reverse-fold remaining flap by opening it and collapsing the tip to the inside.

4. Crease neck along dashed line.

5. Reverse-fold by opening the neck and collapsing the tip to the inside.

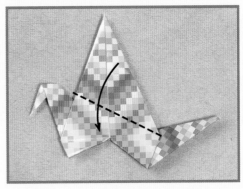

6. Fold wing down along dashed line. Turn model over and repeat.

7. Completed Flapping Crane.

Note: To flap the crane's wings, hold the base of its neck with one hand and pull on its tail with the other hand.

85

How can I use the Fish Base form?

What you need to get started:

Origami paper, 6" square: blue

From this basic form, you can create a balancing act. This "trained" seal props itself up on its flippers and can hold a ball on its nose! This model looks great at a circus- or zoo-themed birthday party.

Seal

Here's how:

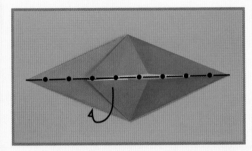

1. Refer to Basic Form VIII: Fish Base on page 34. Begin with a Fish Base.

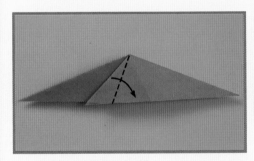

2. Fold model in half so opening is at the bottom.

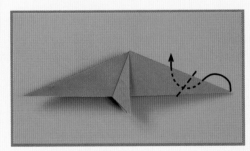

3. Fold upper flap to the center. Turn model over and repeat.

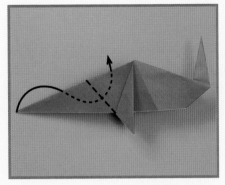

4. Crease along the dashed line and reverse-fold by opening flap and collapsing the tip to the inside.

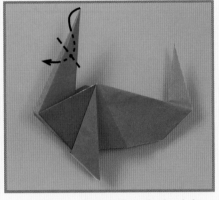

5. Crease along the dashed line and reverse-fold remaining flap by opening it and collapsing the tip to the inside.

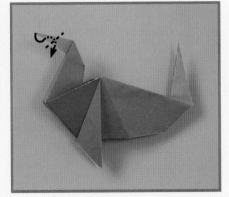

6. Crease neck and reverse-fold by opening the neck and collapsing the tip to the inside.

7. Crease snout and reverse-fold by opening and collapsing the tip to the inside.

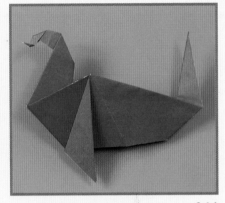

8. Crease nose and reverse-fold by opening and collapsing the tip to the outside.

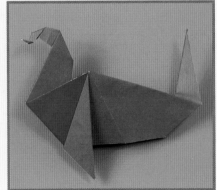

9. Completed Seal.

How can I use a rectangular piece of paper?

What you need to get started:

Craft glue stick
Origami paper, 6" square: double-sided, pink and purple
Rotary trimmer

This colorful crayon motif can be used in a number of delightful ways, from decorating the sides of a canister to embellishing a school-days scrapbook page. You can also punch a hole at the bottom edge and attach a string to create a whimsical bookmark.

Crayon

Here's how:

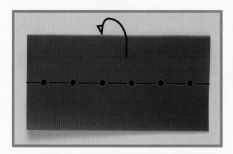

1. Trim origami paper into a 6" x 3" rectangle. Set aside the remaining paper strip.

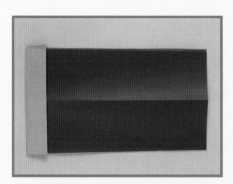

2. Fold paper in half (pink side of paper is inside).

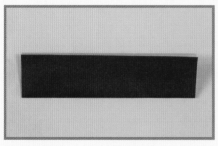

3. Unfold and fold left edge ½" to the right.

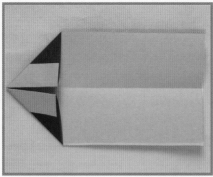

4. Turn model over. Fold top- and bottom-left corners to the horizontal midline.

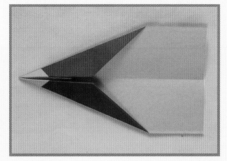

5. Fold top- and bottom-left corners again to the horizontal midline.

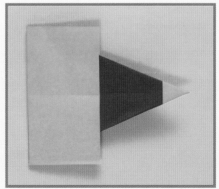

6. Turn model over. Fold left edge to the right.

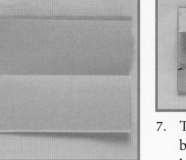

7. Turn model over. Fold top and bottom edges to meet at the horizontal midline.

8. Turn model over. Rotate and adjust side edges so the shaft of the crayon is slightly larger than the slope on its tip.

9. Completed Crayon.

10. From the remaining paper, fashion a stripe and glue it onto the crayon.

Tip

Display your child's school photo in an original way. Simply center and glue the photo onto the shaft of the crayon. Write his or her name and class below the photo and present it to family and friends.

14 project

What you need to get started:

Craft glue stick
Origami papers, 6" square:
blue / purple / white (6)

How do I make a square box?

Be it a sparkling bauble or a sweet treat, you can present that special gift in an extra-special way by placing it inside this origami box. Because you make the box yourself, it can be of any size or color you wish—to suit any season or occasion.

Gift Box

Here's how:

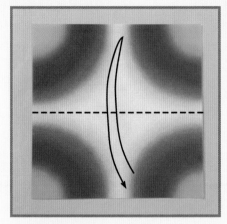

1. Begin with a square.

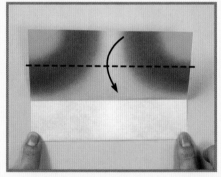

2. Fold in half (right side of paper is inside). Unfold. Fold bottom edge to the horizontal midline.

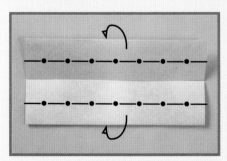

3. Fold top edge to the horizontal midline.

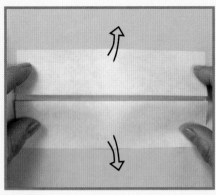

4. Turn model over. Fold top and bottom edges to horizontal midline, pulling flaps out from behind.

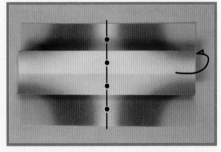

Note: If you were to turn the model over, it would look like this after making the folds.

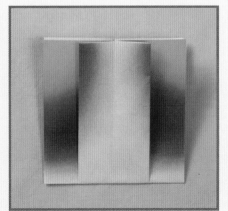

5. Rotate model and fold in half (wrong side of paper is inside).

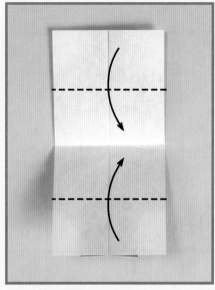

6. Unfold last fold.

7. Fold top and bottom edges to horizontal midline.

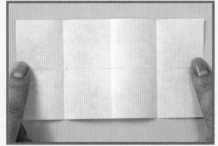

8. Rotate model. Unfold the last two folds.

91

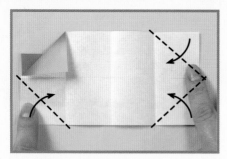

9. Fold top-left corner to the horizontal midline.

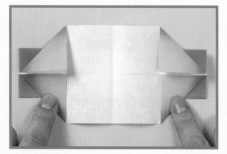

10. Fold remaining corners to horizontal midline, creating two tab ends.

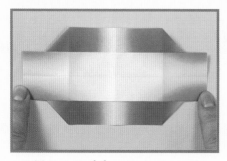

11. Turn model over. Repeat Steps 1–10 to make six models.

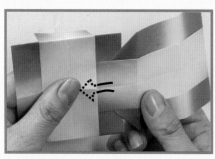

12. Insert one tab end of one model into the side of another.

Note: To help secure the assembly, apply glue to the end before inserting it into the side of other model.

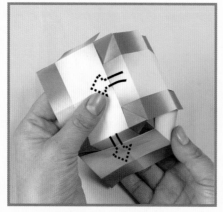

13. Continue inserting tab ends into sides of consecutive models to form a cube.

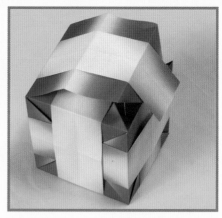

14. Insert a small gift before inserting the last tab end into the side of the next model. Do not glue last tab.

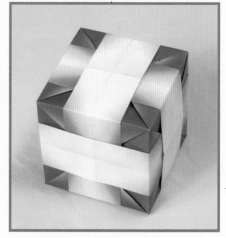

15. Completed Gift Box.

Tip

Mark the tab that will open the box with an origami heart or a note.

How do I make a large-scale project?

You can experiment with different sizes and weights as well as different colors of paper when folding almost any origami project. In this project you will be making a relatively simple form from a large, heavy-weight piece of paper.

What you need to get started:

Craft glue stick
Heavy-weight paper,
    12" square: navy blue

Letter Holder

Developed by Soonboke Smith

Here's how:

Note: To allow for a closer view of the folds, the following photographs show the folding for this project using a 6"-square piece of origami paper.

Be aware that the actual project will look different in relationship to hand placement due to the difference in paper sizes.

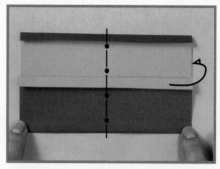

3. Fold top edge of upper flap 1" toward the bottom edge.

6. Rotate model. Fold left and right sides to vertical midline.

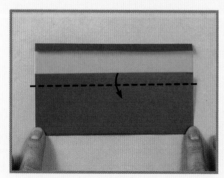

1. Begin with a square. Fold top edge 1" toward the center.

4. Turn model over. Fold left side to the right so model is folded in half.

Note: If you were to turn the model over, it would look like this after making the folds.

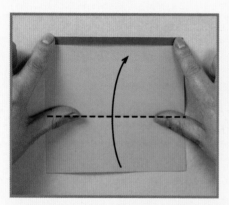

2. Fold bottom edge two-thirds of the distance toward top edge.

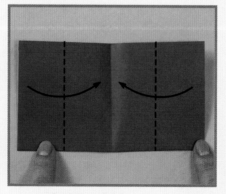

5. Unfold last fold.

7. Place your index finger between layers on the left side and press to flatten.

94

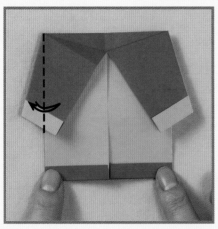

8. Repeat Step 7 for the right side.

11. Glue the flaps onto the back side of the model to secure.

12. Completed Letter Holder.

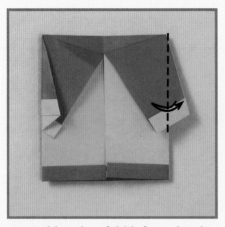

9. Fold and unfold left- and right-points along dashed lines.

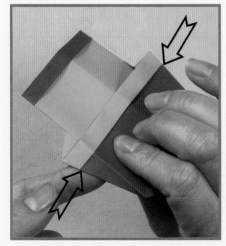

10. Reverse-fold by pushing the previous fold on left and right toward inside of model.

Tips

Use origami papers in all sizes, colors, and finishes to make unique cards to go in your letter holder.

Make a letter holder for each member of your family so each person has their own mailbox. Strengthen your family unity by leaving each other notes of appreciation, encouragement, and even apologies.

16 project

What you need to get started:

Craft glue stick
Mini string of lights
Origami papers, 10"
    square: brown,
    green
Paper punch: round
Rotary trimmer

How do I fold two papers as one?

By layering two pieces of paper—one on top of the other—you can expand the possibilities of your origami crafting and produce more-true-to-life forms and figures.

Pine Tree

Developed by Soonboke Smith

Here's how:

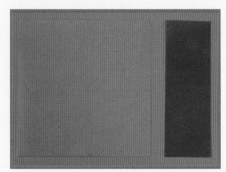

1. Trim brown origami paper into a 3⅜" x 10" rectangle. Position the brown piece of paper on top of one side edge of the green paper. Glue the two pieces of paper together so you can begin with a square.

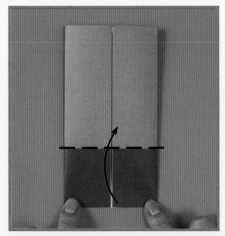

2. Rotate model so brown paper is along bottom edge. Fold in half vertically (wrong side of paper is inside). Unfold. Fold left and right sides to vertical midline.

3. Fold bottom edge one-third of the distance toward top edge.

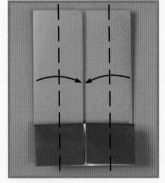

4. Fold the top two-thirds of resulting layer down.

5. Fold left and right sides to vertical midline.

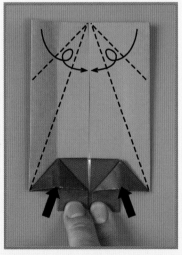

6. Place your index finger between flaps on the bottom-left side and press to flatten. Repeat for bottom-right side.

7. Fold top left and right corners to vertical midline.

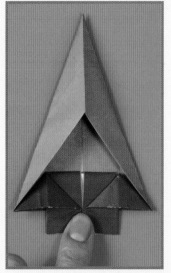

8. Fold top left and right corners again to vertical midline.

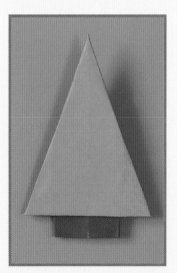

9. Turn model over. Completed Pine Tree.

10. Punch along left and right slopes of tree. Wrap mini string of lights around the tree as desired.

97

"Wishing You Happiness All Through the Year" folded by Soonboke Smith and arranged by Martin Lovato

folded by Geoline Havener

"Sketchbook" quilt developed by Mary Jo Hiney

Section 4: the gallery

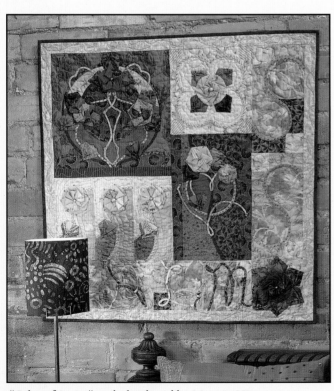

"Calm of Lotus" quilt developed by Mary Jo Hiney

"Lotus Flower" slippers developed by Mary Jo Hiney

As a child, **Geoline Havener** flourished in Hawaii's rich multicultural milieu. She studied oriental art forms at the Honolulu Academy of Arts Museum and Polynesian arts and crafts at the Bishop Museum. However, she says her greatest teachers of traditional Polynesian and oriental arts and crafts were her grandmother, Bo Lin Lee, and the elders in her community.

When Geoline moved to Memphis, Tennessee, she began sharing her rich multicultural knowledge of oriental aboriculture, fine arts, and folk culture with scholars all over the world via the internet. She writes oriental folk culture and instructional articles, from contemporary crafts to ancient horticulture, for a wide variety of publications. One of her favorite pastimes is fusing traditional oriental crafts like origami with contemporary arts and crafts. Geoline is a frequent blue-ribbon and best-of-show winner at the Mid South Fair Creative Arts Competition held in Memphis.

"Madama Butterfly" developed by Geoline Havener

Geoline's son, **Ernie Havener**, is a genius with an autistic spectrum disorder known as Asperger's Syndrome. Since Asperger's Syndrome results in some impairment of sensory perception, origami is used to help Ernie develop fine hand-motor skills and fine hand-proprioceptive sense through the use of various paper thicknesses and textures. Origami has also become a fun way for Ernie to appreciate and learn more about his oriental heritage.

Ernie is another multiribbon Mid South Fair Creative Arts Competition winner in the Havener household. He enjoys fusing origami with his interest in space exploration, architecture, and robotics. The entire Havener family are members of Origami U.S.A.

"Imperial Dragons" folded by Geoline Havener

folded by Geoline Havener

101

"Sketchbook" quilt developed by Mary Jo Hiney

"Frog" developed by Mary Jo Hiney

"Snail" developed by Mary Jo Hiney

Mary Jo Hiney works as a freelance author, designer, and project contributor in the fabric and craft industries, gladly sharing skill-filled secrets gathered over a lifetime of experience. She is an expert seamstress and credits her solid sewing foundation to her mom, who had learned to sew in junior high from a very strict teacher. Mary Jo credits her love for quilting to her sister, Rose. It was Rose, whose love for projects that require detail and precision, who laid the foundation for Mary Jo's knowledge of piecing and quilting some 25 years ago. It was Rose who first took Mary Jo to a fabric store that specialized in quilting fabrics, and it was Rose who helped Mary Jo make her first quilt. What better gift could a sister give?

The fabric origami pieces shown here can be found in Mary Jo's recently published book, *Quiltagami*.

103

"Come Play With Me" quilt developed by Mary Jo Hiney

"Tropical Fish" quilt block developed by Mary Jo Hiney

"Dolphin" quilt block developed by Mary Jo Hiney

"Crane" quilt block developed by Mary Jo Hiney

"Star in Block" quilt block developed by Mary Jo Hiney

"Never-ending Bursting Flames of Passion" developed by Soonboke Smith and arranged by Martin Lovato

Photo by Michael Skarsten

Language teacher and as a substitute teacher at her daughter's elementary school. The children love it when she uses origami as part of her lesson plan.

Some of Soonboke's hobbies include drawing, singing, and working out. She finds that these activities, like origami, all help her to relax. Origami has allowed her to expand her creativity and has taught her patience.

Dedication

To my daughter, Samantha, and my cherished friend, Anthony Rojas. Thank you, Samantha, for all your love and support and for sacrificing our time together to allow me the time I needed to finish this book.

Thank you, Tony, for helping me physically, emotionally, financially, and especially spiritually through this wonderful opportunity in my life.

About the Author

Soonboke Smith was born in Taejon, Korea; one of four children in her family. She grew up watching her mother work with pieces of old fabric—cutting them, folding them, and hand-stitching them together again, transforming them into new finely crafted garments. This time with her mother would later spark Soonboke's interest in Korean Jong ie Jup Gi, or paper folding.

In 1992, Soonboke moved to the United States. She is currently living in Roy, Utah. She has an 11-year-old daughter, Samantha, who is turning out to be quite an origami artist herself. They are proud of their Korean culture and the heritage they share.

Soonboke is an origami instructor at Michael's Crafts store in Riverdale, Utah. During the summer, she teaches an origami day camp for children at the Eccles Community Art Center in Ogden, Utah. She has also worked as a Korean

Special Thanks

Thanks to Linda Orton for introducing me to Desirée Wybrow of Chapelle, Ltd; to Chapelle, Ltd., for giving me this opportunity of a lifetime; to Desirée Wybrow, Cindy Stoeckl, Leslie Farmer, and the entire staff at Chapelle, Ltd., for working with me on this wonderful endeavor; to Kevin Dilley of Hazen Photography for being so kind and making me feel comfortable during the photo shoots; to Martin Lovato, show-room design manager at Jimmy's Floral, for all the outstanding work you did in helping me make my dreams into reality and for all your support and advice; to my doctor, Virginia Moll, for believing in me and encouraging me every step of the way; to Karen Cozier and Marisa De Garlais for supporting me and being there when I need you; to my loving family in Korea, for all their prayers and best wishes for me and the success of this book; and to the good Lord for surrounding me with such talented people and loving family and friends.

"Whisper of Hope" developed by Soonboke Smith and arranged by Martin Lovato

Photo by Michael Skarsten

developed by Soonboke Smith

developed by Soonboke Smith

developed by Soonboke Smith

folded by Soonboke Smith

"Easter Trumpets" developed by Soonboke Smith and arranged by Martin Lovato

Metric Equivalency Chart

inches to millimetres and centimetres (mm-millimetres   cm-centimetres)

inches	mm	cm	inches	cm	inches	cm	inches	cm
⅛	3	0.3	6	15.2	21	53.3	36	91.4
¼	6	0.6	7	17.8	22	55.9	37	94.0
⅜	10	1.0	8	20.3	23	58.4	38	96.5
½	13	1.3	9	22.9	24	61.0	39	99.1
⅝	16	1.6	10	25.4	25	63.5	40	101.6
¾	19	1.9	11	27.9	26	66.0	41	104.1
⅞	22	2.2	12	30.5	27	68.6	42	106.7
1	25	2.5	13	33.0	28	71.1	43	109.2
1¼	32	3.2	14	35.6	29	73.7	44	111.8
1½	38	3.8	15	38.1	30	76.2	45	114.3
1¾	44	4.4	16	40.6	31	78.7	46	116.8
2	51	5.1	17	43.2	32	81.3	47	119.4
3	76	7.6	18	45.7	33	83.8	48	121.9
4	102	10.2	19	48.3	34	86.4	49	124.5
5	127	12.7	20	50.8	35	88.9	50	127.0

Index